THE STARTING POINT LIBRARY

MATHS

Kitchen Maths

THE DANBURY PRESS

A Division of Grolier Enterprises, Inc.

This girl is in the kitchen.
She is setting the table.
How many spoons has she put out?
How many forks will she need?

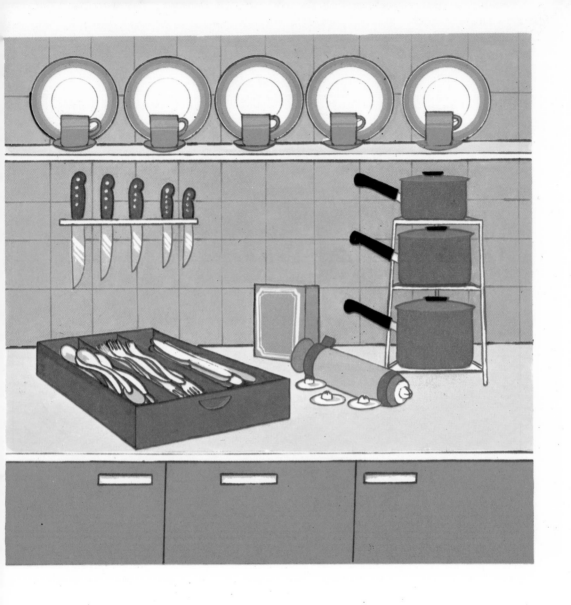

There are many sets in the kitchen.
Can you see a set of knives?
What other sets can you see?
Which set has the least things in it?

3

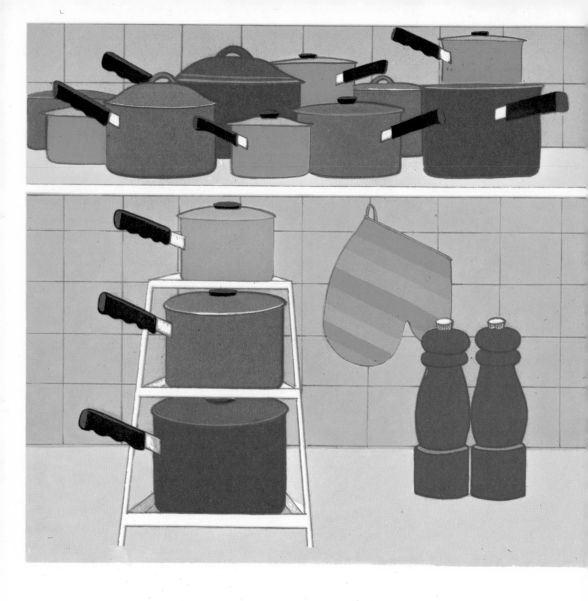

Count the blue saucepans in the picture.
Find the small red saucepans.
Look at the saucepans in the rack.
Are they in any order?

4

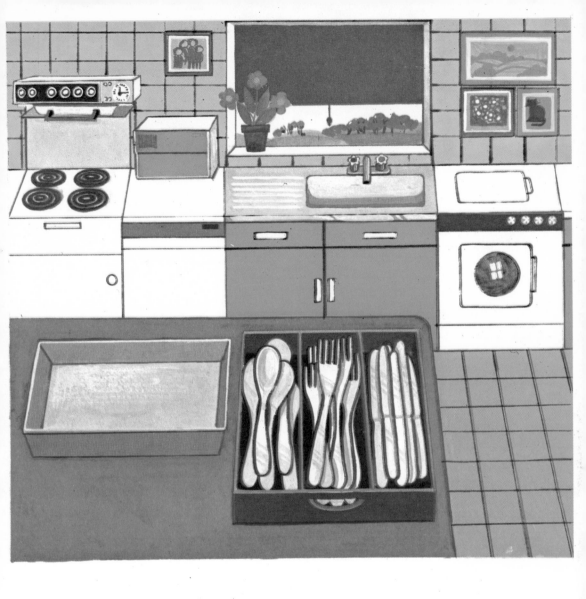

Everything in the kitchen takes up space.
Some of the things are shaped like boxes.
Look at each face of a box.
Do you know what shape they are?

Look at the shapes in the kitchen.
Can you see the rectangles?
Squares are a kind of rectangle.
Can you find the squares?

These children are filling a bowl
with water.
They are using mugs to fill it.
How many mugs will fill your bowl?

Pour a jugful of water into a jar.
Then pour it into a bigger jar.
Is the amount of water the same?
Try this with some other jars.

8

Some machines measure mass.
What is the mass of a packet of sugar?
Try weighing things on a spring scale.

9

Get two boxes of the same size.
Fill one with macaroni
and one with sugar.
Find out which is heavier.

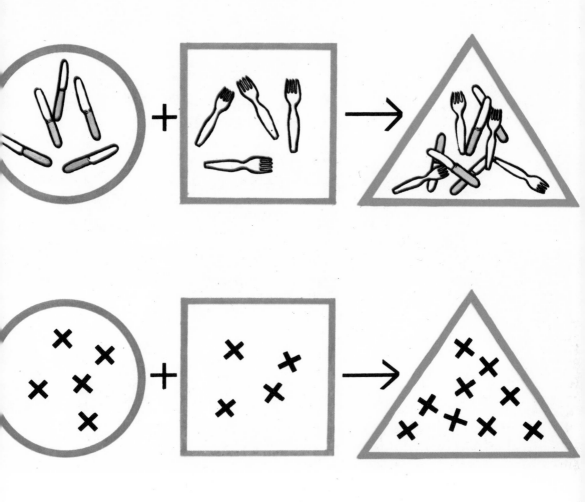

Here are sets of knives and forks.
Count the knives and then the forks.
Add the number of knives
to the number of forks.

Mother is ironing a handkerchief.
It covers part of the table.
The towel covers part of the wall.
Which of them covers more space?

Make some dough.
Cover a plate with dough.
Cut out some shapes from the dough.
Make some long and some short shapes.

Clocks tell us the time.
When you bake a cake
you need a timer.
What does it do?

14

Point to ½ past an hour on a clock.
Measure 1 pint of water.
Can you pour ½ a glass of water?
Find something with a mass of ½ pound.

There are many wheels in the kitchen.
The pastry wheel rolls along.
The beater rotates.
What else do you think rotates?

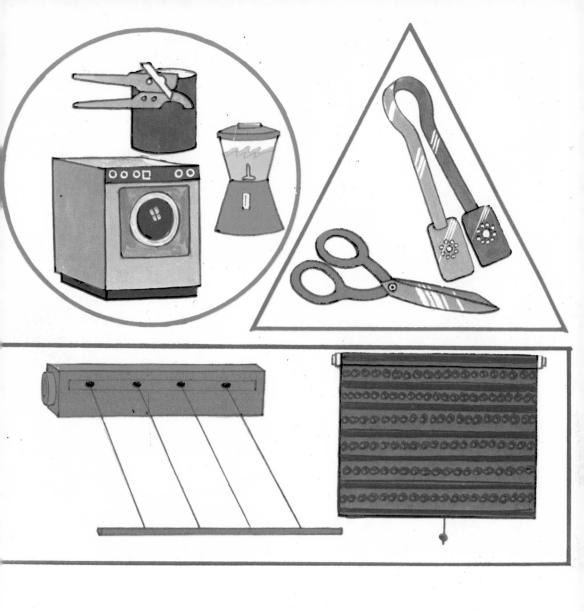

Here are some kitchen sets.
The shade is a kind of pulley.
What else is in the set of pulleys?
Do you know how the other sets work?

17

Here is a set of crockery.
It is sorted into sub-sets.
What is in each sub-set?
Why is the spoon outside the set?

18

Here is a graph of the crockery.
Which set has the least?
Are there more plates than cups?
Can you make a graph of your cutlery?

Look at the lines in the picture.
Most of these lines are straight.
What shapes do the lines
which cross make?

20

Look at all these curved shapes.
Can you find the cylinders?

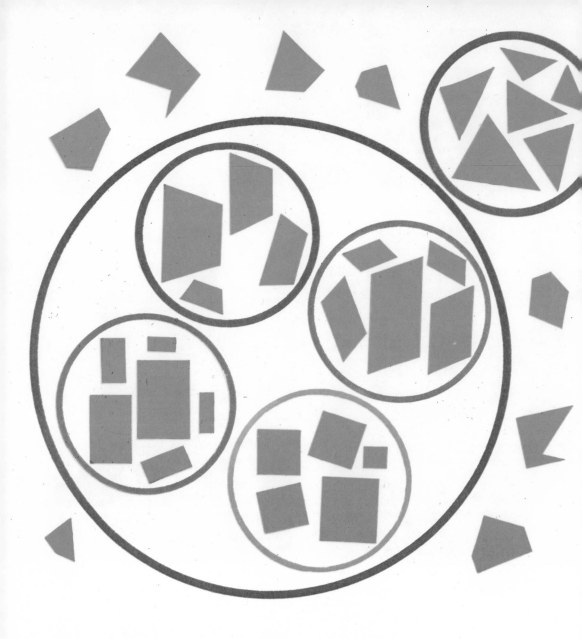

Here are some different shapes.
Can you find the rectangles?
Find the square rectangles.
Can you see the set of triangles?

Tiles cover the kitchen walls and floor.
They make a pattern.
The blind has a pattern too.
Can you make patterns like these?

It is hot in the kitchen.
How do we know how hot the oven is?
How can we measure the temperature?
What is the temperature today?

One boy measures his height on the door.
He can see how he has grown.
Try growing some bulbs.
Mark how much they grow each week.

| more than 1 quart | 1 quart | less than 1 quart |

Collect some jars.
Find those which hold a quart.
How many hold more than a quart?
How many hold less?

Find a bottle which holds a quart.
Can you measure ½ a quart of water?
How much water fills the other bottles?

Index

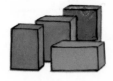